Petoskey Stones: Poems

by

Andre F. Peltier

Finishing Line Press
Georgetown, Kentucky

Petoskey Stones: Poems

This collection is dedicated to my parents
who raised me in Petoskey, MI,
and always kept Northern Michigan in our hearts.

ACKNOWLEDGMENTS

Manufacturing a Snow appeared in *The Writer's Den*
Six Feet Under appeared in *Alternate Route*
Snow Angels appeared in *Madrigal Press*
The Batman of Petoskey appeared in *In Parentheses*
Gazing Waterward appeared in *Madrigal Press*
Hockey Night in Emmett County appeared in *The Write Launch*
Kim Fields at a Pistons Game appeared in *Bullshit Mag*
When War Broke Out appeared in *The Great Lakes Review*
Ghosts of Ypsilanti appeared in *Provenance Journal*
The Ebullient Signpost appeared in *Open Leaf Press*
Northern Lights appeared in *Outcast Press*
On a Clothes Line in Norther Michigan appeared in *Wingless Dreamer*
Hard Lessons from Dawn Donuts appeared in *Alternative Milk*
After Soccer Practice appeared in *Substantially Unlimited*
Petoskey Sun Set appeared in *Paddler Press*
Those Hexagonal Corals appeared in *Dynamis Journal*

Publisher: Leah Huete de Maines
Editor: Christen Kincaid
Cover Art: Julie A. Stratton
Author Photo: Thomas William Ulch
Cover Design: Elizabeth Maines McCleavy

Order online: www.finishinglinepress.com
                    also available on amazon.com

Author inquiries and mail orders:
Finishing Line Press
PO Box 1626
Georgetown, Kentucky 40324
USA

Contents

Manufacturing a Snow Day

As the temperature dropped,
we filled buckets and
poured water on the road.
A better plan
had never been designed.
Ice on the asphalt,
we knew,
meant the school bus
would never be safe.
Unsafe conditions
were what we needed most.
Trip after trip,
relay after relay,
we ensured the slickness
of the street.
Our scheme was
foolproof.
No school bus could
survive the frozen
wasteland
that was our neighborhood.
No bus driver
in his right mind
would risk it.
Mr. Johnson would
have to make the call.
The drifts weren't enough,
we were certain.
The blizzard
coming in from Wisconsin,
blown across Lake Michigan,
needed our guidance.
We couldn't trust nature
to do what had to be
done.

The weekend
was for sledding, skiing,
skating.
A Monday in our desks
would be such a waste.
Who could blame us?
We would be hailed as
heroes.
A three-day weekend
at the end of January.
For all the kids in town,
Terrier Lane would be a
tundra.
For all of the kids in town,
we were bringing
freedom and peace.

In Monday morning math class,
we couldn't comprehend
what went wrong.
Our infallible plot
had failed.
Our valiant effort was forgotten.
I guess we didn't use enough
water.

Six Feet Under

"All true stories begin in a cemetery" [1]

We played Hide-n-Seek,
Kick the Can, & Bloody Murder
everywhere we went.
Neighborhood games with thirty kids,
in department stores
hiding behind racks of blouses
or bathing suits,
in parking garages
weaving in & out of cars,
pillars, stairways.

Saturday mornings
were soccer mornings.
The field was adjacent to
St. Francis Cemetery.
When the older kids kicked the ball
we kicked the can,
we crouched behind
the tombstones.
The small cedar groves disguised
our eternal souls while we waited
for a twenty count, "ready or not
here I come," &
"Olly Olly Oxen Free!"
We ran 'round that graveyard
without a thought to the saintly dead.
Our freedom was true & everlasting.

One October morning,
I found the perfect spot.
A hole in the ground:
right angles, smooth sides & deep.
Who leaves a hole just laying around?
I jumped in; no one could find me.
Perfection six feet down.

I had to call for help
once it was clear that
I couldn't get out.
The other kids got our parents,
& while shaking his head,
my father pulled up
the post-modern Lazarus
who left only footprints
upon that hole's sandy bottom.
The other parents
tried to hide their disgust…
their laughter.
I didn't understand the concern.
It was just a good hole.
Who doesn't love
a good hole?

That afternoon,
my mother & I
went grocery shopping.
We drove past the cemetery
& saw a crowd around
my hiding pace.
They were looking down,
probably questioning
the child's footprints at the bottom.
Probably considering the dirt
kicked down while I attempted to
scramble up.

"Did another kid get
stuck down there?" I asked.
"Not exactly," mom replied.
"Not exactly."

1 Zafon, Carlos Ruiz. *The Shadow of the Wind*. Translated by Lucia
Graves, Penguin Books, 2004.

Cedar Swamp

The river winds
through lowlands,
through cattails, pitcher plants,
Joe Pye Weed.
It falls and winds
through the dogwood,
rudbeckia, skunk cabbage
before joining the lakes
and ultimately the great oceans.

Smiling salamander
on the banks,
under his leafy shelter,
watches the gentle flow,
listens for the squawk
of the mallard
and the screech
of the red-tailed hawk.
Leopard frog sings and swims.
And still the unstill river winds.

The fallen cedar spikes stab
the open curve below
Dead Man's Hill.
The ox-bow beyond Chestonia
awaits the stately return
of her stately harrier.
Haliaeetus leucocephalus
hides in bent birch
and the river falls and winds,

ever searching for the outlet,
for its companion molecules
to bubble and sink
and swirl.

Snow Angels

The northern slopes
of Michigan,
blanketed in quiet
snow,
were for sledding
and sledding only.
We ducked under
electrified
fence and barbed wire.
We pulled
saucers and Flexible Fliers
through knee-deep drifts,
tromped to the
frozen creek,
watched rabbits and
deer forage frozen food.
We lounged
along the banks of
the icy creek
making snow angels:
arms and legs akimbo.

Those deep impressions,
like the foot-prints of
the white-tailed rabbits,
hoof-prints of
the white-tailed deer,
slowly faded as the winter
gave way to spring,
or as the next February
storm erased them
from hillsides and leafless
forest floors.
Those carefree days
also erased
like the angels.

Like old photos,
memories curl and fade,
melting into history,
on the northern slopes
of forgotten days.

The Batman of Petoskey

He stalks the streets
of Northern Michigan
in his cape and cowl.

When the superstitious
cowardly lot creep through
town, he is there.

On patrol, on the lookout
for the good of the
common man,

The Batman of Petoskey,
hero to us all,
is ever-vigilant.

How could a man
so pure be
wrong?

How could a man
of such intentions
become the laughingstock?

Investigating the serious
crimes, he solves the
serious crimes.

On the scene before
police or sheriff,
he always gets his man.

Gazing Waterward

I
It was up north
when I was
younger.
We lived on a bluff
overlooking the bay.
From our deck
everyone said
"What a nice view you have,
you must
gaze
for hours at the
water."
We watched silently
the sailboats.
We reached back and
cast our gaze
waterward
like fishermen
and we saw freighters
come and go
talking of the cement plant
day and night.
The plant is gone now;
morphed
into something shiny
and new.
Watching the sails
like Columbus and
Captain Kidd.
Semaphore signals to
the shoreline.
Over the wide
expanse of land,

over the trees
over the highway
we gazed for hours
and it was ours;
lake and rocky coast,
day and night,
ours forever
from the top of that
hill.

II
In the lazy long hours
of the afternoon sun,
we rode down the hill
to follow the stream
to the falls
and out into the bay.
Left and right, all paths
lead us waterward.
We knew not
leaches
nor the rushing cars
overhead
as we crouched
under the road,
through the culvert,
tunneling,
tunneling like moles
like ants to a picnic.
Michigan was our swimming
hole.
There we were naked
and free.
Free
like Tom and Huck,
free like Jim.

People would ask
what we did there,
but we couldn't say.
We could not stay.
It was invisible
from the top of the hill,
seen and unseen,
unseen and unknown.
No one could take it from us.
We were connected to
Niagara
and the seas.
We knew this stream,
shallow and
thoughtless,
was young like us.

Hockey Night in Emmett County

Saturday afternoons
we met at 7-Eleven
with our gear and
frozen fingers.
Fifteen of us crammed
in the bed of an F-150,
the cap our only shield
from the screaming snow.
Across northern Michigan
this motley assortment of
fourth-grade fiascos
traveled to Charlevoix, Cheboygan,
Alpena.
The ponds solidified by
the Solstice;
even the big lakes were frozen.
Mackinac Island only accessible
by snowmobile:
a row of Xmas trees lined the way
across the straights.

Rogers City was the coldest though;
it was fifteen below,
yet they made us play.
The pick-up truck
skated over the old Trunkline
through Fingerboard, Afton,
and Onaway.
We fell out of the Ford,
loaded down with
bubblegum and Slurpees
(Slurpees warmer than the wind),
to don our shin-guards, sweaters,
and sticks.
We wore stocking caps
under our helmets
to no avail.

We doubled our socks
to no avail.
Ears numb from biting
February skies,
we took the ice
and stood our ground.

An hour later,
heading home again,
shivering and forlorn,
we licked our wounds
as tongues froze to hardened
iron skin.
That night,
drinking cocoa
and sharpening skates,
we dreamt of grand glory
under the frigid twinkling of
Gemini and Auriga.
"Next week," we prayed,
"Next week we will be
victorious."

Kim Fields at a Pistons Game

Marcus lived two houses down.
At 15 years old we were inseparable.

After school, we watched *Rap City,*
Yo MTv Raps, He-Man.

We read comics: he *Green Lantern* and *X-Men,*
me *Batman* and *Star Trek.*

We road to the record store and listened to
Public Enemy while eating spaghetti in our bedrooms.

One night, his parents got us tickets
to a basketball game.

At The Palace of Auburn Hills,
we cheered for Zeke, Worm, Microwave.

In front of us sat Kim Fields, in all her glory;
she laughed and watched the game.

Turning to me, she smiled.
Her dreadlocks and leather jacket so cool.

Tootie smiled at me, and, during that third
quarter, my life was perfect.

When War Broke Out

On the edge of the gully grew
three old apple trees,
stately and gnarled.
The remnants of some
ancient
grove or orchard,
at one time sweet and juicy,
now the size of golf balls
and sour as the day was long.
We climbed and ate none-the-less.
Hours we spent
in those trees.
Hours we spent hiding
in the leaves.

In spring, the blossoms bent boughs
and filled the air
with our stately perfume.
Like snow after a
blizzard,
white blooms blanketed the canopy
and consumed creation
with autumnal nectar.
But it was in summer
we climbed.
It was during those long,
golden days
we perched with robins and jays
atop the greenery.

We were drawn to those lofty treetops,
all of the children
in the neighborhood.
Compelled to make it
higher
than the day before,

higher than our friends.
Some were giants
while others were a tangled mess
of honeysuckle or lilacs.
We conquered them all,
Hand over hand.
But those twisted apples
always beckoned.

Sometimes, in early fall, war broke out.
Ten kids within the trees;
ten in the adjacent field...
and the apples were
launched
volley after volley.
Hours passed
as we played at combat.
No winners or losers,
just bruised children
and bruised apples.
In the end, mice and worms
would feast as we were called
home at dusk.

Ghosts of Ypsilanti

Ypsilanti casts long shadows
from Woodruff's Grove
to The Norris Block.
Ghosts of Union dead
return to the ancient depot
and haunt the students,
the cyclists, the poets
of reconstruction hellfire dawn.
When those nervous boys
convened on River St.
before their southern odyssey,
when the bright-eyed youth
boarded those cars
heading to blood and destruction,
they boarded those cars
with smiles on their lips
and bayonets in their eyes.
South Mountain
and The Siege of Corinth
saw the red rivers of Ypsilanti,
the red deluge of Washtenaw County.
Those boys choked
the vertebrae of the Confederacy;
they cut off the head
of the Chattanooga Timber,
its fearful rattle
lonely and lost.
When Ypsilanti froze
in the ice of '97,
the ice of '02,
we stayed warm under the blankets
of Huron River stones,
under the blankets
of catfish, crappie, and carp.

When we were buried
in the snows of '99,
we stayed warm
with the beer of Depot Town
and the pancakes of Cross St.
Those ghosts of Union dead
kept us warm as they haunted
the bell-tower
and rang their haunted song,
lonely and lost.

Towards Little Cedar Lake

Walking through Waterloo,
thinking of Napoleon
& the end he met on those
fields in Flanders.
The little general,
home from exile for
one last hurrah.
He sat upon his horse
& even the Seventh Coalition
craned their necks
to catch a glimpse.
The Wallooners stood by
as his 72,000 men marched
to doom.
Our Waterloo is not Belgian;
we hike those trails
west of Ann Arbor every fall,
the same trails for ten years.
There's an old beech tree
with names, initials, dates,
& we mark it each October
as we count our trips
to the bog & our cold
autumnal mornings.
The leaves are changing
or have already fallen.
The brown of the earth
and the brown of the forest
intersect as the brown
of our boots cuts through the trails.
Sometimes the streams are frozen
& crack as we step across.
Other times, the boardwalk is flooded
& the mud is ankle-deep.
We traverse that mud
& our boots go
splootch splootch splootch

as they break the suction & break
the surface over & again.
The bog itself, quaking and delicate,
sits at the end of the observation deck.
Pitcher plants, ferns,
sphagnum have coexisted with
the rabbits & deer since the last glaciers
left southern Michigan.
Their retreat carved our peninsula,
carved the history of the Great Lakes.
The old oaks, some of which have stood
since before Bonaparte left Elba,
since before the Peninsular Wars
& his great Russian quagmire.
Walking to the bog,
we are all a bit like Napoleon,
we have all escaped exile
only to return.
He died on St. Helena;
we will die in our cubicles,
on our smart-phones,
with our lattes in our laps,
but those moments approaching
Cedar Lake, approaching
the quaking bog,
those are the real moments.
As he looked out over that battlefield,
as his end was near,
he dreamt of walking to the bog
one last time,
he dreamt of leaving it all behind,
of trading his epaulets & bicorne
for another chance
to see the Labrador Tea,
another chance to carve
his name in an old beech,
another chance to crack

the frozen stream &
dream of Elba.

The Ebullient Signpost

When Deputy Don rode
into the sunset
with a song and a smile,
we wore ten-gallon hats
& sat side-saddle
on the arms of our father's
Lay-Z-Boy recliners.
When we clanged pots & pans
with neighborhood dogs
as the boys of summer
won another pennant,
when the young willow
twisted and tangled
the septic pipes
into new & disgusting
contortions,
we dug deep in the field
& covered the hole
with grass to trap bears,
tigers, marauders,
the old woman
from down the street.
She fell into our trap
& twisted her ankle.
We laughed as she
limped away.
Fair warning:
"Walk our trails—
face the consequences."
Like Robin Hood or Zorro
or Grizzly Adams,
we hid beneath
the Queen Ann's Lace,
beneath the monarch
butterflies,
& laughed as
she limped.

We tromped through
the woods
with stolen Marlboro Reds,
white Zebra Cakes,
& warm Labatt's Blue,
we climbed the tallest tree
& peeled the bark
to reveal the true grain
of the giant beast.
From our perch,
we could see the rainbow
sails of rainbow ships
upon the rainbow bay.
Sunlight glistened, reflected,
blinded us,
but we never averted our eyes.
When the fireworks of three towns
filled the sky,
we never averted our eyes.
When the shaving cream
& water-filled condom balloons
splashed our faces,
we never averted
our eyes.

With popcorn, cold pizza,
warm Faygo Rock n Rye
for midnight snacks,
we played five-card draw.
The French-Canadian
poker chips
had been tucked into
Great-Grandmother's dresser,
behind her knitting,
her teeth, her hairbrush
& her forgotten
ninety-three years

of horse-drawn dreams.

They emerged to settle
our scores.
We watched Joe Bob Briggs
& Count Zappula.
Imported Italian erotica,
black and white horror trash:
signifiers of adolescent
rebellion,
the ebullient signposts
of the freedom
of youth.

Northern Lights

We lugged lawn chairs
to the cornfield
with our case of Busch Lite.
We sat huffing
gasoline, smoking
Camel straights,
realizing our future
began that night.
As our heads cleared
from the fumes,
overcast midnight skies
cleared too.

We stared in awe
as the dissipating clouds
gave way to early
October Aurora Borealis.
We passed the gas-can
around again,
inhaled deeply,
and saw our collective
tomorrows
writ upon that crazy
neon north.

On a Clothes Line in Northern Michigan

On the bluff
overlooking
Lake Michigan,
the winds came in from
Chicago, Green Bay,
Traverse City.
We hung the sheets
in the yard, and
like the wind chimes
in the trees,
like the seagulls on
the wing,
they fluttered and danced.
The breeze of daybreak
blew those soaked
sheets shining.
We placed them back
on our beds
and dreamt of neon
northern lights
over the hills of
Harbor Springs.

Beware of Leprechauns

Winding west of Washtenaw, on
Rte. 12 we discover the old ways.

Rte. 12 uncovers the overgrown
ice cream stand and mini-golf course.

Once, a go-cart track raced through the hills;
now the track is wild and neglected.

And the dinosaurs of The Irish Hills haunt
those woods while they watch the day-trippers,

the lonely fathers, the work-a-day commuters
bouncing between Jackson and Ann Arbor.

The Old Sauk Trail carried Indians from
the straights to the base of Lake Michigan,

from Detroit to Chicago. Threaded between
 the lakes and the bluffs of Lenawee County,

the stagecoach brought gamblers, schoolmarms,
ministers, and bankers as they sought a new beginning.

For five days, they rolled, rocked, bounced down
the old trail. In The Irish Hills, they found a bed

and a bowl of stew. In The Irish Hills, they found
safety and comfort. In The Irish Hills, we find

the forgotten ruins of post-war holiday bliss.

Hard Lesson from Dawn Donuts

He pocketed a pack
of Marlboro Reds
from the counter
at the local donut shop.

We biked to the woods,
sat under a tree,
lit one off another,
and finished them all
inside of twenty
minutes.

"You look green,"
she told me
as I moaned frozen
floating, spinning
like a land-lubber at sea
above my blankets.
"You stink of tobacco,"
she continued.

"I don't know
what you're talking about.
How could this be?
I would never touch
those things.

Excuse me.
I think I'm going to be

sick."

Dissolving Daylight Sundae

Covered in sprinkles,
the horizon melts,
drips down our hands;
we lick it clean.
The soft-serve line of sunset,
five kilometers from our
sinking feet,
turns shades of pink,
orange, yellow
as whipped cream
clouds float
overhead.

We stood at the curve
of the bay,
skipping stones
into that sweet vanishing point,
into the long herald of night.
Seven skips we counted
before it sank to
the holy depths.
Seven skips towards
the melting
sundae of
dissolving
daylight
dreams.

After Soccer Practice

We shed our shin guards
on the sidelines
and hoofed it to the bend
beneath the Howard St. bridge.
Parents chatting
in the parking lot
as we dove into
the cooling waters
holding adolescence
for another
August afternoon.

The Bear River creeps
north from Melrose,
in essence, just a smelt stream,
but for us,
spectacular and pure.
For us,
our private
fountain of youth.

In the Dunes

She laid on her beach towel,
face-down with her top
untied to avoid
the dreaded tan-lines.
I hid behind the dunes
and gawked.
She must have been home
from college
for the summer:
an older woman…
bronzed by the sun,
exotic, alluring,
a perfect tableau vivant.
She was my everything
for that one afternoon.
From my sand dune sanctuary,
she couldn't have known
I was there.
Emerson's invisible eyeball,
I saw all but remained
unseen.
A twelve-year-old creeper
dreaming of egalitarian
poetry,
reading the world
in her curves.

As she packed up,
carefully placing her radio,
her towel, her water bottle
into the canvas beach-bag,
she smiled,
"Be careful in the dunes, kid,
your mom is probably worried
about you by now."

Petoskey Sun Set, 4 July 2010

Sands blown in
from Lake Michigan
since the Pleistocene thaw.
Those dunes welcomed Anishinabek
home from hunts,
home from celebrations of
The Three Fires
in Leelanau, Keweenaw,
Mackinaw.
They rowed from St. Joseph,
Manitoulin, Wikwemikong
to rest at the mouth of
The Bear River.
They netted salmon
at the falls where those rays of light
met the great inland sea.
Later, the train came
bringing settlers and farmers
from the dread white south.
Overlooking those falls
from The City Park Grill,
Ernest drank his Death
in the Afternoon.
He shipped out to Europe
and injury from the base
of those dunes.

And on those dunes,
my son sat, among the grass
and rugosa pebbles.
He nursed his lemonade
leaning on his lawn chair.
He awaited the fireworks
as the golden sun
turned pink and red
through western twilight haze.

Like Hemingway
and the early hunters
who made those pine woods home,
he silently watched
as the light gave way
to another endless night.

Those Hexagonal Corals

In shallow Devonian seas,
those hexagonal corals
grew and died,
silent and forgotten.
Epoch after epoch,
they waited.
Epoch after epoch,
those hexagonal corals,
fossilized and still,
drowned in frigid Michigan
waters.
After the trek of the Manitou,
after the rise of dunes,
those hexagonal corals
were awakened by the rumble
of the ice.
As glaciers receded,
the fossils found their way
shoreward.
Towards Charlevoix,
Bay View, Harbor Springs,
they plotted their path
through Little Traverse Bay.
As Chief Pet-O-Sega
surveyed the headwaters of
The Bear River,
the bubbling springs of Walloon,
the sunset coast of Sturgeon Bay,
those hexagonal fossils
churned the mucky depths
and rolled towards shore.
John Herman drank his whiskey
and slipped into the shoals,
he road those rocks
east to haunt Waugoshance Light.
Shoveling coal and playing jokes,
John Herman knew the fossils.

While Stanley Smolak stacked
his river stones
and carved the driftwood,
he looked across to
Beaver Island
and saw the future,
the past in all its ugly elegance.
The former Devonian seas,
now glacial scars,
deposit the fossils along
the margin of the bay
where they sprout like daffodils
along quiet Grasmere.
The holy Petoskey Stone
is collected and polished,
polished and sold:
trinkets bought and
forgotten,
collecting dust in drawers,
attics, shoeboxes.
The beacon that is the
holy Petoskey Stone:
siren for all who brave
the seance of Emmet County
shorelines.

Andre F. Peltier (he/him) grew up in Petoskey, a small town in northern Michigan. He is a Pushcart and Best of the Net nominated poet. He earned his Bachelor's Degree in 1998 and Master's Degree in 2000 in Literature from Eastern Michigan University where he has taught ever since. As a Lecturer III, he teaches Poetry, African American Literature, Detective Fiction, Science Fiction, Afrofuturism, and writing. He lives in Ypsilanti, Michigan with his wife, his children, their dog Daisy, and their two turtles: Dr. Watson and Mrs. Hudson. His poetry has recently appeared in various publications both online and in print. His debut poetry collection, Poplandia, is a collection of pop-culture based poems. In his free time, he obsesses over soccer, his own team and the sport in general, as well as comic books. He is willing to read any comic even tangentially connected to Gotham City. He wishes to thank Sara Peltier for her constant love and support, Julie A Stratton for the use of her amazing artwork on the cover, and all of his friends and colleagues who have offered advice and critiques over the years.

Twitter: *@aandrefpeltier*

Website: *www.andrefpeltier.com*

www.ingramcontent.com/pod-product-compliance
Lightning Source LLC
Chambersburg PA
CBHW020221090426
42734CB00008B/1160